TODAY I SAW A PROPHET

KATHLEEN H. BARNES & VIRGINIA H. PEARCE

Library of Congress Cataloging in Publication Data

Barnes, Kathleen H
  Today I saw a prophet.

  SUMMARY: Identifies biblical prophets from Moses to Peter, explains the role of prophet and lists the men who have served in this capacity for the Church of Jesus Christ of Latter-Day Saints.

  1. Prophets (Mormonism)—Juvenile literature. 2. Prophets—Juvenile literature. [1. Prophets (Mormonism) 2. Prophets. 3. Church of Jesus Christ of Latter-Day Saints] I. Pearce, Virginia H., joint author. II. Title.
BX8643.P7B37   230'.9'3   77-4986
ISBN 0-87747-646-2

T

Today I saw a prophet.

He smiled at me and shook my hand,
and I felt warm inside, because I
know a prophet is a man who speaks
for God and leads His people.

A prophet is a light
in a dark world.

Long ago, even before Jesus was born into the world, there were prophets.

Moses was an ancient prophet.

Moses led his people out of Egypt.
He heard the voice of God
in a burning bush.
He received the Ten Commandments
on a tablet of stone.

Moses spoke for God.
Moses was a light to his people.

"…a prophet shall the Lord
your God raise up unto you
…like unto me; him shall ye hear
in all things whatsoever
he shall say unto you."
—*Acts 3:22*

Noah was an ancient prophet.

God told Noah to build a boat
so that all the righteous people
and the animals could be saved
when the floods came.

Noah spoke for God.
He was a light in the world.

John the Baptist
was a special prophet.
He lived in the wilderness
and baptized people who came to him.
He told the people
that Jesus Christ would come.

He spoke for God, saying that a light
would soon come into the world.

And Jesus did come into the world.
He taught us how to live, and because
of His life, we can live again with
Heavenly Father.

He established His church here
on the earth and then He was crucified.
He died for us, and was resurrected
on the third day.

Then Peter became head
of the Church of Jesus Christ.
Peter had been a fisherman,
but Jesus had told him
to become a fisher of men.
Peter was a light to the people.

After the apostles were gone,
the light began to flicker.
Then, for many, many years,
there was no prophet.
The people did not know about God
and what He wanted them to do.
All was darkness.
There was no light.

One spring morning,
not too many years ago,
a boy went into the woods to pray.
He wanted to know about God,
and he saw Him and heard Him
in a beautiful vision.

The boy's name was Joseph Smith.

God taught Joseph Smith
and Joseph taught the people.
He became the first president,
prophet, seer, and revelator
for The Church of Jesus Christ
of Latter-day Saints.
He could speak for God.
There was light again
in a dark world.

Brigham Young was a prophet.
Like Moses, he led his people
on a long journey to a new home.
When he saw the Salt Lake Valley
he said, "This is the place."
He spoke for God.
Brigham Young was a light
to his people.

Other prophets followed
Brigham Young—

John Taylor
Wilford Woodruff
Lorenzo Snow
Joseph F. Smith
Heber J. Grant
George Albert Smith
David O. McKay
Joseph Fielding Smith
Harold B. Lee

They all spoke for God.
Each was a light
in a dark world.

18

Today Spencer W. Kimball
is the president, prophet, seer,
and revelator for The Church
of Jesus Christ of Latter-day Saints.

In 1943, President Kimball
became an apostle, and for the next
31 years, he worked closely
with the prophets. He learned
about Heavenly Father and what He wants
His children to do.
When President Harold B. Lee,
the prophet of the Church, died,
the Twelve Apostles met together
in the temple. After praying,
they all knew that Heavenly Father
wanted Spencer W. Kimball
to be the prophet.

Like other prophets,
President Kimball speaks for God.

Every year in April and October,
there is a general conference
of the Church. Leaders from all over
the world meet in Salt Lake City.
They learn and they listen—
listen to the prophet speak.
They know that the prophet
will tell them what Heavenly Father
wants them to do.

Like other prophets,
President Kimball works hard.

He goes to many meetings.
He meets with important people
of the world and tells them
about Heavenly Father's church.
He meets with missionaries.
He wants them to try harder.

Each Thursday President Kimball
attends a special meeting in the temple
with the Twelve Apostles.
They sing, they pray, and they talk
about doing the work Heavenly Father
wants them to do.

Our prophet lengthens his stride.
He says, "My life is like my shoes—
to be worn out in the service
of the Lord."

26

Like other prophets,
President Kimball prays.

As President Kimball goes to meetings,
works, studies, travels, and teaches,
he always has a prayer in his heart.

He prays that all people everywhere
will keep the commandments.

Today I saw
President Spencer W. Kimball.
Like Moses, like Joseph Smith,
and like all other prophets,
he speaks for God.

He is a light in our dark world.
I will follow him.